I0510248

The Secret Diary of a Mystery Shopper

True Customer Service Stories through the eyes of a secret shopper: The Good, The Bad and The Exceptional

Claire Boscq-Scott

This book is for sale at
http://leanpub.com/thesecretdiaryofamysteryshopper

This version was published on 2020-09-03

Leanpub

This is a Leanpub book. Leanpub empowers authors and publishers with the Lean Publishing process. Lean Publishing is the act of publishing an in-progress ebook using lightweight tools and many iterations to get reader feedback, pivot until you have the right book and build traction once you do.

© 2020 Claire Boscq-Scott

Tweet This Book!

Please help Claire Boscq-Scott by spreading the word about this book on Twitter!

The suggested tweet for this book is:

I just bought The Secret Diary of a Mystery Shopper, check it out for yourself, it's no longer a secret!

The suggested hashtag for this book is #secretdiaryofamysteryshopper.

Find out what other people are saying about the book by clicking on this link to search for this hashtag on Twitter:

#secretdiaryofamysteryshopper

Also By Claire Boscq-Scott

Contents

CONTENTS

Introduction

Setting up a Mystery Shopping business

You know when you meet someone for the first time and they ask you, so what do you do Claire?? I absolutely love watching people's reaction when I say:

'Well, I have the best job in the world! I get paid to get massages, get nails done, eat in restaurants and sleep in fabulous hotels...'

Wouldn't you love to get paid to shop??

I have indeed the best job in the world, not because I get paid to shop but because I help businesses improve their service delivery, increase their employees' engagement and customer loyalty, have a thriving business and exponential growth. I feel like the bees, well like the Queen Bee, of course, and just like those remarkable small size creatures, who have been helping our planet's ecosystem since the dawn of time, it is my mission to help businesses to thrive...

I have always worked in the hospitality industry. Born in Paris, I moved to the South of France with my parents when they opened their first restaurant. I was seven at the time. That was when I first started carrying plates, and when the passion for all things relating to hospitality and customer service began. When you grow up in that environment, you either love it or you hate it; fortunately, I absolutely loved it! I loved the interaction with the people, I loved witnessing them enjoying good food and wine and I loved welcoming them back time and time again.

You probably won't have heard of a very old French film called 'L'aile ou la cuisse' (The Wing or the Thigh). It is a 1976 French comedy film directed by Claude Zidi, starring Louis de Funès and Coluche. If you haven't watched it, go and find it - especially if you like French films. It is very funny. It's about the life of a food inspector whose son doesn't want to follow in his steps. I remember being a little girl and wanting to be a Michelin Inspector, too. I thought it would be amazing to go and eat in amazing restaurants and sleep in wonderful hotels. After two decades being in the receiving hand of Mystery Shoppers, auditors, assessor, secret shoppers, I would have never thought that my little girls' dream would become a reality...

Between 2008 to 2009, whilst working at L'Horizon Hotel & Spa, we used to have monthly mystery guest visits from a UK company. I thought, shouldn't we be doing this with a local company? A company who would really understand our local needs? After doing some research, I realised there was a gap in the market for a similar service with local knowledge. This excited me. It gave me the impetus to leave my secure job and pursue this idea. In the summer of 2009, I sold my house and used the profit to set up on my own business, to provide a service that filled this gap. And so, the next chapter of my life began.

Starting my business Claire Boscq-Scott[1] The Busy Queen Bee[2] during a recession was a notably bold move; a mad move perhaps, as some people suggested. However, it is often during such times of adversity that successful businesses rise; especially when they are devoted to helping enterprises improve their customer service. We were certain that, it was perfect timing to establish a customer-focused business during this recession, when looking after and retaining your customers was vital and, frankly, more important than ever.

The vision of my business has always been to help businesses thrive and grow their profitability by delivering exceptional customer experiences. Indeed, if the local businesses thrive, so will the local

---

[1]https://www.claireboscqscott.com
[2]https://www.busyqueenbee.com

economy...

So, there I was: a little French girl with big dreams, taking the leap of faith and hungry to make a difference. When starting a business, you have to get your name out there, so I attended all the networking events I could. I was here, there and everywhere; breakfast meeting, lunch and evening cocktails. I remember walking into my first Institute of Director lunch at The Grand Hotel, in Jersey; a room full of men. It was quite scary, I have to say. I ran into the bathrooms to give myself a little pep talk, a bit of lipstick, straightening my shoulders out. I said to myself, 'Come on, Claire. You can do this.' And I did.

There's a saying by Richard Branson:"If somebody offers you an amazing opportunity but you are not sure you can do it, say yes – then learn how to do it later!" Well, I was talking to everyone, explaining what mystery shopping was and how it would improve their services, until one day I received a phone call. Someone wanted to work with me, but could I do Pan Islands? Jersey, Guernsey and the Isle of Man... I didn't think twice about it and excitedly said yes. Then, as I put the phone down, I thought: 'how am I going to do that?' And that was the beginning of my Mystery Shopping adventure. I was ready to buzz.

Very quickly, I had to recruit Mystery Shoppers in different locations. It was funny when I remarked to a friend that I was just like the queen bee, and all my shoppers were my little bees, who go off and work for me and return with the pollen - the results for our clients. A couple of years later, I came across Davina MacKail, who became my coach. Our conversations were always so inspiring and, from them, "The Busy Queen Bee" was created. We worked together on the rebrand - the story behind the bee, the brand colours and what they represent, the refocus on my core services and what I wanted to achieve. It was a transforming year for the business, and BQB was finally born!

You know when people ask you what you do for a living? Well,

I was really proud to be able to say: I am a Mystery Shopper, and I get paid to go into restaurants, hotels, and shop! Wow - that's the kind of job anyone would want, no? So for the last decade, we have performed thousands of visits, worked with over 20 different industries, from car to retail, financial services to hospitality, helping them in many ways to improve their service delivery. It's been an amazing journey and every new project was creating new experiences, new stories, new learnings, and I was so proud to have several of my clients winning Industry Awards, retaining their 5 star ratings and increasing the brand awareness and profit because of the work we did together.

The notion of 'The Hive' really appealed to me. I am amazed at the complexity and intellectual capacity of bees and have created over the years methodologies, aligned to the bees' incredible work conduct, which can be applied to customer service strategies. I have used the beehive analogy in my first two books, Thrive with the Hive[3] and Thriving by Caring[4] as it is so powerful, I am giving away a free E-Copy of Thriving by Caring, in the downloadable resources on the book webpage[5]

But, I have had this little idea in the back of my head for a few years: my idea of starting a new book, that could help businesses even further by telling real customer service stories: the good, the bad and the exceptional. It is a secret diary, so no business name will be mentioned. However, one or two stories I have used are not Mystery Shopping ones, but ones that the whole wide world has heard of, and I thought they'd be good additions to this book. Most of these stories are my personal observations, or stories that I have picked up along the way, and stories from people who can't help but tell me their experiences.

I want this book to be very helpful, as well as a useful reference,

---

[3]https://www.claireboscqscott.com/books/thrive-with-the-hive/
[4]https://www.claireboscqscott.com/books/thriving-by-caring/
[5]https://www.claireboscqscott.com/books/the-secret-diary-of-a-mystery-shopper/

you can also download from the book webpage[6] all the resources mentioned in this book. I want to get people thinking - that includes businesses, employees, and customers. It's funny when someone tells me a story about customer service, because it's not just one story they will tell me, but two, three or four of them, as they feel they must tell me the good, the bad, the ugly and the (so many) exceptional ones. It may resonate with you and if you have a story to share, feel free to send it over...

---

[6]https://www.claireboscqscott.com/books/the-secret-diary-of-a-mystery-shopper/

Time to re-evaluate

2019 started with some mind-blowing news, when I received an email to announce that I was listed No.5 on the Global Customer Service Guru List. I was listed No.5 Global Guru for three consecutive years, which is amazing, as this is decided by a vote by people. So thank you so much to all who voted for me last year!

I also decided to create a programme, which would bring all of my three decades of expertise into one place, where I could really make a difference to businesses. I could work with them not just of their service delivery, but looking at their Culture, their environment, their people and their customers, called Caring Service Culture Programme. It is following my new ECX Method™ Employee & Customer Experience Method[7]. It is a real transforming process, balancing caring soft skill - such as NLP, feng shui, emotional intelligence and mindfulness - to the hard logic of the analytical research approach, with a set of metrics within this framework to measure the impact on your business. We can work hand in hand during that whole year, to move the dial and quantify the value of the programme, aligning everything to Employee and Customer centricity.

Following this, I went for a couple of trips to Manila in the Philippines, which opened up a brand new market. The Philippines has one of the fastest GDP growth in Asia, at around 6,4%. There is no wonder why so many businesses there are looking at improving their service delivery, their people and their businesses growth. I have been a keynote speaker at The Franchise Asia Conference, The National Retail Conference & Expo, at the HR Summit, at the Women Connected and also at the Philippines Association of

---

[7]https://www.claireboscqscott.com/cx-methodology/

Professional Speakers (PAPS). Wow, it felt amazing sharing my expertise on stage in front of so many people. The buzz from Manila was in me. I was looking forward to going back in 2020, if not before!

My trip to Split, in Croatia, was to bring me more than just a meet up with my friends from Mystery Shopping Professional Association (MSPA) and attend the annual conference, but also the meeting with Natalia Ugren, who is going to become - in a couple of weeks - my new Licensee in Slovenia BQB CX Method Practitioner and Trainer[8]. Friday 13th was a lucky one for me, as I was surrounded with customers, shoppers, family & friends to celebrate 10th Business Anniversary and also the launch of my new Perfume, Eau d'Abeille[9], which is inspired by my obsession with getting businesses to connect with their people and customers at an emotional level. It's another one of my crazy ideas which made a right buzz.

And then March 2020 arrived...
And our whole world went into the most incredible crisis... #covid_-19 had hits us all!

In 3 days, I had lost 100% of my clients. All my speaking gigs and training sessions had been cancelled and confinement started!

The same thought came back to me as when I started - surely, businesses will need to seriously focus on engaging their employees and on retaining every single customer they have during the pandemic, but businesses were fire-fighting themselves and customer service was the last of their worries.

However, it is in those extraordinary times that we have to take stock of what we do, why we do and how we can help our clients. So, I did just that. It wasn't an easy decision, but I decided to retire from running my Mystery Shopping operations. The toughest decision I had to take for a long time, but I want to focus on helping

---

[8]https://busyqueenbee.com/bqb-cx-slovenia/
[9]https://www.claireboscqscott.com/eau-dabeille-your-beejou-perfume/

businesses on their Employee and Customer Experience Strategy[10] to create a bigger impact on their businesses improvement, by coaching, consulting and supporting them on their CX journey.

I also want to focus on training employees around the world and developing a Learning & Development online training platform, which would bring different types of training, customer service, and of course, but moreso, the core principles of being a caring person and delivering exceptional customer experience. The BQB CX Institute[11] brings International Experts in their fields who have developed specific programmes to give people the tools to bring out the best of themselves, their world and their business, so they can be happy and deliver exceptional customer experiences in a compelling and lively way. It inspires them to extend their own skills and develop new ones, which has a transformational affect in themselves and in their organisation.

And finally, whether or not I can travel, I get such a buzz by sharing my passion and energy on virtual or real stages, delivering my Keynote Presentations[12] inspiring audiences around the world and spreading the crucial importance of CX (Customer Experience) and EX (Employee Experience), sharing knowledge through the stories in this book, so businesses can be enthused and empowered to make the necessary changes in their businesses and thrive!

---

[10]https://www.claireboscqscott.com/cx-methodology/
[11]https://bqbcxinstitute.org/
[12]https://www.claireboscqscott.com/speaker-customer-experience/

The Good, The Bad and The Ugly

There's a famous Western film called "The Good, the Bad and the Ugly", released in 1966, directed by Sergio Leone. It stars Clint Eastwood as "the Good", Lee Van Cleef as "the Bad", and Eli Wallach as "the Ugly". I love the analogy and thought it would be a great way to divide the book, with one little twist - replacing "the Ugly" with "the Exceptional", so we can celebrate the exceptionally positive stories that await you! That is because exceptional breeds exceptional and let's celebrate more positive stories than the ugly ones...

1. Why Mystery Shopping
2. The Good
3. The Bad
4. The Exceptional
5. The End

I hope you will relate to those stories and share them with your employees; use them for training, developing new standards, making changes in your service and actually providing - consistently - your customers with an unforgettable experience every time they walk through the doors.

So, here we are! Let's get started... I hope you will enjoy reading the book as much as I've enjoyed writing it. Without further delay, let's get on to the first chapter: Why Mystery Shopping.

Why Mystery Shopping?

Seeing The Bigger Picture

Service is intangible - customers' recollection of the transaction is their reality, their attitudes & feelings, their physiological state. It will help them to decide if they want to do business with you again. We seek pleasure and avoid pain, so tend to return to companies that meet or exceed our requirements and avoid the ones that cause pain.

Customers will have their own expectations of what they expect you to do. Their expectations are rarely passed on to you. However, if you don't meet them, the customer may conclude that you have failed. Once you have identified those expectations they can be carefully handled, changed or adjusted.

How would you describe your customers to your friends? There will be positive words; however, there are also likely to be some unhelpful views/words that need to be considered.

Are you unconsciously putting up barriers? So why do we have different perspectives of a situation? Why might we act differently in the same situation?

Internal representation of external events

Not everybody sees the world in the exact same way. Information goes in through our senses and then we all delete, distort and generalise based on our attitudes, values, beliefs etc... We have our own map of the world!

How we see things and how our customers and our staff see things can be entirely different. A vital component in optimum customer service is having empathy for the various points of view of ALL stakeholders involved in the business. We must assess the perspective of both our internal and external customers to be able to see the bigger picture of where we should be headed in terms of delivering an optimum customer experience. As such, it is only when you look after the people; your internal and external customers, during, before and after, and look at both points of view that you can deliver excellent customer service at all levels.

So, what are the **30 benefits for a company to deliver exceptional customer experiences**?

1. Increase profitability
2. Increase number of customers through their doors
3. Increase customers' feeling valued
4. Increase customers' loyalty
5. Increase repeat business
6. Increase referrals & recommendation (word of mouth)
7. Increase customer satisfaction
8. Increase customers' experience
9. Increase shopping basket size
10. Increase brand awareness and loyalty
11. Increase of positive online reputation
12. Increase emotional experience
13. Reduce customer complaints
14. Reduce negative comments on social media
15. Increase employee engagement
16. Increase employee performance
17. Increase employee wellbeing at work
18. Increase employee job satisfaction
19. Increase employee confidence
20. Increase employee loyalty and pride of their job
21. Reduce employee churn
22. Reduce on Advertising cost
23. Reduce recruitment fee

24. Reduce employee sick days
25. Get an edge on the competition
26. Cut price war with competition
27. Add value to customers
28. Stay in business longer and stronger
29. Happy customers, happy employees, happy boss!
30. Ultimately, it will improve the local economy as a whole!!

This is why I live to inspire businesses to deliver exceptional Customer eXperiences, because the whole world would benefit from it!!

Measuring your service delivery, why?

Because you just 'can't manage what you don't measure'. It is an old management adage that is still very accurate and used today. Unless you measure something you don't know whether it is getting better or worse, you can't manage for improvement nor can you celebrate success.

Why Customers leave?
Well according to a survey by CustomersThatStick, 82% poor customer service! and John Gattorna, a visiting professor at Macquarie Graduate School of Management, published the following figures on why businesses lose customers:

- 68% they perceive you are indifferent to them
- 33% consider switching after just a single instance of poor service
- 14% poor product quality
- 9% price
  And that 5% increase in customer retention can increase a company's profitability between 50 & 75%!

You need to measure those activities or results that are important to successfully achieving your organisation's goals. Key Performance Indicators (KPI) is a measurable value that demonstrates how effectively a company is achieving key business objectives.

The KPIs differ depending on the organisation, it may be:
* A percentage of its income that comes from return customers
* A customer service department may have percentage of customer

calls answered in the first minute
* A monthly leads or prospects
* A net promoter score, etc... you get the idea!

Happy customers means happy employees and vice versa...

Measure to manage, measure to celebrate success:
* Measure what's important
* Publish your metrics and benchmarks
* Reward people for achieving and exceeding their goals
* Identify your gaps and do something about it...

And then start over...

Measuring your service delivery means that you can really give the support to your team to improve the customer experience, pinpoint how your customers are feeling and how emotionally connected they are to your brand, and that altogether you are following your business vision. This is the difference between surviving and thriving.

> **Measure service to find what your employees are doing right, and celebrate it.**

Measuring, how? Mystery shopping

Measuring your customer service tells you where you are now and how you measure up against your competition. This important benchmark helps you to set your strategy for the future, there are many aspect of market research and one of the methods to measure customer service is mystery shopping.

Why, as a business, should you use mystery shopping to improve your customer experience?

Well it isn't a difficult question to answer:
* you can't be in your business 24/7
* you can't be in 2, 3 or 20 places at once
* you can't improve if you don't get feedback
* you can't celebrate success
* you can't manage what you don't measure
* you don't know if you are following your business vision

So mystery shopping provides objective quantitative and qualitative feedback about your customer experience at one moment in time.

Mystery shopping isn't about picking on staff; it isn't like "The Big Brother House" (a game show in which a group of contestants, referred to as HouseGuests, live in a custom-built "house" constantly under video surveillance.) where people are watching you until you make a mistake. It is about understanding your level of service, either good or not so good at any given moment. It is about celebrating excellent service and looking at "gaps" when the service isn't so good. Why are your employees not giving excellent service at all times? Well, perhaps you haven't trained them correctly, perhaps they haven't been told what they need to do, or it could be an environment issue. Mystery shopping will give you feedback which you can then act on.

A mystery shopper is someone who has been trained specifically to go, anonymously, into a shop, restaurant, cinema, any business really which has contact with customers (which in my eyes, is every businesses), for the purpose of observing and measuring customer service, product quality and the environment of the establishment in general.

Before performing a visit, the shoppers are given details about what is expected of them, and the full questionnaire which they will need to fill in. Having understood the full briefing, the shoppers will then serve as the eyes and ears for the clients.

After completing a visit, the shoppers will submit their evaluation in a detailed report. Many mystery shopping companies publicise mystery shopping as an easy and fun thing to do: "Be paid to shop", but this is far from true. Being a mystery shopper requires many qualities and is certainly a serious business. They will need to have an eye for details, be able to write quality reports and have a very good memory too.

I have been very lucky to have had an amazing team of just over eighty Mystery Shoppers, who were all professionally trained and efficient and performed thousands of visits over the years. They could work within a retail or hospitality environment, call centres, or to the specific needs of financial services.

The Mystery Shopping Professional Association MSPA[13] offers shoppers a certification, so if you are looking to become a mystery shopper, this is a great way for you to get qualified through our representative body. Also, if you decide to put a programme and want the help of a company, of course, I can help you develop your programme if you want to do it yourself! However, if you wish someone else to do it for you, make sure they are members of the MSPA. At least you'll know you are working with professional

---

[13]http://ow.ly/Wpxj6

companies who follow MSPA ethical conducts and standards and you can be sure they will do an excellent job for you.

20 benefits of a Mystery Shopping programme:

1. Monitors and measures service performance
2. Increases customer loyalty, download 80 customer retention ideas in the resources on the book webpage[14]
3. Increases employee performance
4. Monitors legal health & safety requirements
5. Improves customer retention
6. Makes employees aware of what is important in serving customers
7. Reinforces positive employee/management actions with incentive-based reward systems
8. Provides feedback from front line operations
9. Monitors facility conditions - asset protection
10. Ensures product/service delivery quality
11. Supports promotional programmes
12. Audits pricing & merchandising compliance
13. Allows for competitive analyses
14. Compliments marketing research data
15. Identifies training needs and sales opportunities
16. Educational tool for training & development
17. Ensures positive customer relationships on the front line
18. Reinforces employees' integrity
19. Increase internal and external loyalty
20. Ultimately increase profit & business growth

Once you have decided to use mystery shopping, have clear objectives. What is it exactly that you would like to know?
Is it the general feel of your shop? Is it the selling techniques of your staff or the cleanliness of your toilet? Look at areas that you know

---

[14]https://www.claireboscqscott.com/books/the-secret-diary-of-a-mystery-shopper/

may already have issues, as those are the areas you may want to start with...

Before the programme is implemented, ensure everyone in the company understands that the ultimate purpose of the mystery shopping exercise is to improve the specific behaviours that will create customer delight and have a positive impact on sales and profitability.

Promote the benefits of mystery shops, such as:

- Discovering whether customers are receiving consistently superior customer service at every location
- Identifying gaps in training needs
- Aligning company-wide focus on improving the customers' experiences
- Share exactly what types of questions will be on the mystery shop (or even the exact questions if this doesn't put the shoppers' anonymity in jeopardy)
- Be very clear that the purpose of the mystery shop programme is NOT to criticise, assign blame, or publicly embarrass anyone, and the results of mystery shops will NEVER be used as a reason for punishment

Another great way to further encourage positive buy-in from customer-facing associates is to offer some kind of reward to those who get exceptionally high scores on their shops.

If the benefits of a mystery shopping programme are communicated effectively, all employees should embrace mystery shops as an irreplaceable way to help them succeed by truly understanding what their customers experience. EVERY shop should be seen as an opportunity to more deeply understand exactly what customer delight-driving behaviours look and sound like, and EVERY shop should be used for recognition and/or for positive, constructive coaching.

How you measure, is as important as, what you measure.

How to set up a mystery shopping programme?

Before rolling out a mystery shopping programme, you need to set some clear expectations. What are you looking for, what do you want to achieve when reading the reports?

The Waggle Dance

The Waggle Dance talk was first noted by Aristotle around 330 BC. Because honey bees are social insects that live in a colony, they have to communicate with each other. Honey bees do this by using odour cues, food exchanges and certain movements so they can share important information about food sources. Honey bees perform a group of movements, called the "waggle dance talk", which is a particular figure of eight dance. They do this to inform other worker bees of the exact location of the food source. Some of these locations can be up to five hundred feet from their hive, the speed and distance of the movement conveys the distance of where the food source is so other bees can find it.

When I first looked at the dance pattern, I couldn't stop thinking about this virtual CX cycle I kept talking about, and suddenly it just all made sense. I thought the analogy of the "waggle dance" was just perfect to use in any business to work on any project, so a Mystery Shopping programme will have 4 steps:

1. Assess: determine what is to be measured, why you are doing this programme, what are the objectives
2. Develop: the programme, design your questionnaire, determine what type of evaluation method is to be used, such as on-site visits, hidden video, audio recording, and online interactions, etc...

3. Implement/Train: roll out the programme internally
4. Measure: roll out the programme externally

And then start again:

1. Assess the results
2. Develop new strategies, SMART objectives, you can download how to develop SMART objectives in the resources on the book webpage[15]
3. Implement/train
4. And measure again...

You see the virtual cycle??

Questionnaire Design

An effective questionnaire will allow you to distinguish delighting behaviours from very good or fine behaviours, as well as dissatisfying behaviours from customer-detracting behaviours. This is critical to the success of your programme. You need to develop processes which allow you to capture feedback in a non-subjective manner while still offering performance behaviour distinction where it matters most.

For the sake of accuracy, the questionnaire must be short enough for the shoppers to remember all of what is being asked and not beyond the scope of what is realistic to remember, distinguish, or document. As a general rule of thumb, limit your questionnaire to 30 questions or less. To maximise value, make sure your shop questions are aligned with internal training, focused on actionable and crucial criteria that distinguish your company from your key competitors, and measure the specific behaviours that have the highest impact on creating customer delight and loyalty.

---

[15]https://www.claireboscqscott.com/books/the-secret-diary-of-a-mystery-shopper/

Scale

Each of your questions can be divided into two broad types:

- When a question has two possible responses, we consider it **dichotomous**. Surveys often use dichotomous questions that ask for a Yes/No, True/False or Agree/Disagree response.
- Questions that attempt to measure on an interval level. One of the most common of these types is the traditional one-to-five rating (or one-to-seven, or one-to-nine, etc.). This is sometimes referred to as a **Likert response scale.**

Using a rating scale in survey responses help add another layer of information. Scaled responses are more realistic, more human, and more accurate.

Sometimes you have to ask the employee one question in order to determine whether they are qualified or experienced enough to answer a subsequent one. This requires using a filter or contingency question. For instance, you may want to ask one question if the respondent has ever used this particular hoover and a different question if they have not.

Scenarios

Once the questionnaire is set up, you will script common scenarios:

- Do you want the shopper to purchase an item which has just arrived in your shop?
- Do you want the shopper to make a complaint?
- Do you want the shopper to enquire about a specific promotion you have just rolled out?

The main thing is to keep it simple and realistic...

Mystery Shoppers performing the visit

Once the questionnaire is set up and the scenarios are prepared, the mystery shopper will make enquiries and observations according to the specifications of each project, noting specific details and measurements about the location and level of customer service provided. The shopper then submits a report; most providers have an online service where clients can review the findings. The report will then be edited and checked before you have access to the final results.

The next part, and the most important and interesting part of a mystery shopping programme, is the reception of the results - the analysis and identification of your gaps and following it through with actionable steps.

> **What do you expect the mystery shopping programme to fix, change, or improve?**

Mystery Shopping online training course

Over the years, I realised that a lot of the small businesses couldn't really afford to use my services and this is why I decided to create a Mystery Shopping online training course, so ALL businesses can benefit from the results of a Mystery Shopping Programme. Ok, it is important to remember that putting a Mystery Shopping programme by yourself can have an impact on your results. Imagine having a friend coming into your establishement and having to give some feedback on her sister it may not be completely bias...

Some reasons why doing it internally can give you false results:

- the person may know the other person so they will feel they can't really say what happens because they are their colleagues or they know them
- they may give you over positive feedback because they 'like' you
- or over critical because they don't...
- they may not be able to give you detailed information because they are not trained to look at specifics
- may not remember what you asked to measure and miss elements
- they may not be able to relate to their conversation with your staff in an objective manner
- they be recongnised, because you have sent the same person a few times, no rotations has been done
- they may not be the right profile for your typical customers and may not give the right feedback
- it may take you a lot of time to find people, train them and manage them

So, in the previous chapter, I have given you an outline of what a programme should look like, now you can learn how to develop and roll out a programme yourself, by following my step by step method, and start seeing the change in your business.

Want to know more check out the Mystery Shopping online training course[16] now!!!

Using professionals probably will save you time and money in the long run, and give you better results, remember always use a MSPA member...

---

[16]https://bqbcxinstitute.org/courses/mystery-shopping-online-training-course/

 ## Case Study - Office Depot's President on how "Mystery Shopping" helped spark a turnaround

When I first started my business, I was sent a great story about mystery shopping which I keep referring to. The story is about Kevin Peters, President of Office Depot, a US stationery company, who was performing mystery shopping every month and were getting top results every time. However, the company's profit wasn't growing and he just couldn't understand why.

Here is his story:

The office products retailer was measuring customer service using metrics, such as the cleanliness of bathrooms, that didn't drive sales. Its new president is trying to fix that by retraining the staff and transforming the company.

"When I became the leader of Office Depot's retail stores in the United States, in 2010, the first thing I tried to do was figure out the meaning of a puzzling set of facts. Our sales had been declining, and although that's not unusual in a weak economy, they had declined faster than the sales of our competitors and of retailers in general. At the same time, the customer service scores our third-party mystery-shopper service was reporting were going through the roof. This didn't make any sense. How could it be that we were delivering phenomenal service to our customers, yet they weren't buying anything?

To understand these contradictory data points, I decided to do some mystery shopping myself. I didn't wear a suit. I didn't wear a blue Office Depot shirt like the ones employees wear in all our U.S. stores. Instead I wore a faded pair of jeans, a T-shirt, and a baseball cap. I didn't tell anyone I was coming to visit, and in most cases I didn't let anyone know afterward that I'd been in the store. What I wanted was to experience Office Depot in the same way our customers do. Over the next several weeks I visited seventy stores in fifteen or more states.

At each location I followed the same routine. First I pulled into the parking lot and just watched customers go in and out for a few minutes. When I went into the store, I'd spend twenty to thirty minutes observing what was going on. I'd talk to customers in the aisles and as they were leaving the store. Some of the most interesting conversations took place when I followed people out who weren't carrying shopping bags and asked them why they hadn't bought anything. Some of them gave me an earful.

I could tell you a lot of stories about the things I saw, but two scenes stand out in my mind. In one store I watched an employee argue with a customer about whether or not we carried a calculator that her son needed for first grade. An employee arguing with a customer, it was unbelievable.

At another store, I parked and saw an associate leaning up against the brick facade smoking a cigarette. Meanwhile, customers were walking out without any bags. This employee did nothing, he just watched them leave empty handed. At that point I had a tough decision to make: Should I blow my cover and alert the store manager, or should I stay silent? I sat in the car a few minutes, thinking it over. Finally I decided, I just can't let this go.

I went into the store and looked at the stanchion that stands at the front of every location, displaying the name of the manager and his or her picture. Guess who the store manager was? Yes, the guy smoking outside the store. So I went up to him and introduced myself, and we had a good long talk. He was ashamed of his behaviour, and he was sweating during the conversation. He promised he'd do a better job of taking care of customers, and I promised to keep in touch. Even today we exchange e-mails every month to discuss his performance.

Get In, Get Out...

During most of my visits, though, I managed to stay incognito, and I came away having learned a big lesson: Our mystery shopping scores were correct. You know what was flawed? Our scoring system. We were asking the wrong questions. We were asking, are the floors clean? Are the shelves full of inventory? Are the store windows clean? Have the bathrooms been cleaned recently? Think about that for a moment: How often do you go to the bathroom while shopping for office supplies? It turns out that customers don't really care about any of that. Those factors don't drive purchases, and that's why our sales were declining. It would be easy to blame our associates for ignoring shoppers, but under the system we'd built, they weren't doing anything wrong. They were doing exactly what we'd asked them to do, working to keep stores clean and well stocked instead of building relationships with customers.

My conversations with customers gave me three insights into how we should transform our business to become more competitive: One, we had to reduce the size of our stores. They were too large and too difficult to shop in. Two, we had to dramatically improve the in-store experience for our customers. That meant retraining our associates to stop focusing on the things our existing system had incentivised them to do and focus on customers instead. Three, we had to look beyond office products to provide other services our customers wanted. They wanted copying, printing, and shipping. They wanted help installing software and fixing computers. We needed to expand our offerings if we were to remain relevant to our customers.

Talking directly with dozens of customers also reminded me of a cold, hard fact: They have many choices. Office products are a $300-billion industry, and the top three players, Staples, Office Depot, and OfficeMax, account for less than ten percent of that. Approximately sixty-five percent of our customers are small and mid-size businesses, and buying office supplies doesn't add value to what they do. It's a chore. They want to get in and get out, they care about convenience above all else.

What We Say Matters...
Office Depot wanted to dramatically improve its customers' in-store experience. That included making the questions employees asked more open-ended.

Less Stocking, More Selling...
On the basis of that feedback, we began to transform our business. It's probably one of the most challenging journeys I've taken in my life. We started by designating two test stores, one in Chicago and one in south Florida.

Many of the changes we made were done behind the scenes, in parts of the business that customers don't see. We altered the way our supply chain operates so that we could accept deliveries from vendors even when no one was in the store to sign in the merchandise. We began separating stock onto U-boats (the narrow stocking carts we use in aisles) assigned to different parts of the store and delivering the U-boats to an optimal spot, marked with an X on the floor, to minimise the labour required by associates to stock shelves. We also divided the store into zones and began having the same associates stock the same sections repeatedly. Becoming expert in one area of the store allowed them to restock faster, reducing labour.

Many people think that in order to improve service, you need to hire more frontline workers. But in fact, by finding ways to reduce the time employees spend on functions such as stocking shelves, we've been able to repurpose their time for selling to customers. Each of our stores employs 18 people on average; by finding ways to work smarter, we've been able to save 80 hours a week, the equivalent of hiring two full-time salespeople but at no added cost.

Once our associates had more time to serve customers, we needed to ensure that they knew how. We simplified our sales process from five steps to three, it's now called ARC, for "Ask, recommend, and close" and trained them to implement it. We taught them to ask customers open-ended questions. Our research indicated that in certain departments, such as furniture, sales go up by more than hundred percent when associates with really good product knowledge are assigned to those zones. So in addition to sales training, we invested in product training.

When a retailer delivers poor service, many people are quick to blame the employees. In my experience, it's more complicated than that. We have 22,500 associates in our retail organisation; one of the things we did as part of our change programme was to have every one of them take a test built on the Myers-Briggs Type Indicator to help us understand their skills, behaviours, and attributes as they relate to serving customers. An interesting thing we found was that we'd been hiring people who were most comfortable with their backs, rather than their bellies, to the aisle. Roughly one in five associates preferred performing tasks on merchandise over interacting with customers. A challenge we faced in rolling out these initiatives was how to help those workers become comfortable with the ARC culture or, frankly, to help them find other meaningful jobs within the company if they couldn't acquire the right selling skills.

Smaller Is Better...
You can't drive changes like this overnight. Our business has been around since 1986, and that's a long time for employees and customers to establish expectations and behaviours. These changes won't be completed in the next month or the next quarter maybe not even in the next year. In addition to the two "lab" stores in Chicago and Florida, we've rolled out 30 pilot stores, and we're seeing encouraging evidence of an improvement in sales. We're also hearing positive anecdotal feedback from customers and associates. There has been a dramatic improvement at the store where I caught the manager smoking outside: Today it is one of the top performers in the company. We hope that by the end of 2011, 325 of our stores will be utilising the new system.

We've also made progress in shrinking the size of our stores. Today they average 24,000 square feet. We've already had success with new stores of 15,000 to 17,000 square feet. We are introducing a small-format store that's about 5,000 square feet. It carries only 5,000 SKUs compared with 8,500 SKUs in our traditional stores but because they're our most popular products, they represent 93% of what we sell in a traditional store. This format will allow us to be in downtown markets like New York City or in remote markets where we wouldn't consider putting a large-format store.

As we work to make these changes, I still try to visit our stores as frequently as possible. It's really the only way you can know how your business is doing. You have to see how customers are being treated, and you can't rely on reports or scores or hearsay you have to experience it yourself. If you think your company is doing well with customer service, ask yourself, Am I really sure? Do I know what the customer experiences?

What I pay attention to most of all is how many people are leaving the store without a shopping bag. I'd be glad if people came to our stores to browse, but this is not a browsing industry, people are shopping with a very specific purpose in mind. If they don't make a purchase, something has gone wrong. If we can reduce this "balk rate" by just 10%, it will have a meaningful impact on both our top-line revenue and our margins.

You also have to make sure you're measuring things that really matter to customers. I can tell you from first-hand experience what happens when you measure the wrong things. I always try to remember that we need our customers more than they need us and we'd better act like it.

Our mystery shopping scores were correct, but our scoring system was not. We were asking the wrong questions. We found that we had been hiring people who were most comfortable with their backs, rather than their bellies, to the aisle."

The Good

When someone think they have spotted a Mystery Guest!

Very early on, I organised a trip to another British Isle to recruit mystery shoppers.

I stayed in a hotel, which had a lounge-bar so I could meet all of the people who had applied for the mystery shoppers' job. All day, I had people coming in and out to speak to me to become a mystery shopper. The bar staff were coming to clear my table and I could notice they were eavesdropping!

In the evening something odd happened, the bar staff must have heard me talk about mystery shopping and passed it on to the management. As I sat down for dinner in the restaurant and was served as if I were a queen, at one point I could see the Chef and the Manager looking at me from behind the kitchen door. It was so funny.

The next morning, I was welcomed by Mr Drinkwater, The Hotel Manager, all suited and booted. He asked me how my stay was and gave me his business card, and asked: how did we do?! I responded with, how did you do what? He said to me, aren't you an Hotel Inspector? I was laughing inside and said, not that day, but gave him my card and told him to call me if he wanted to have some mystery guests visits done - I could help!

The biggest challenge a mystery shopper faces is being identified as a mystery shopper. This can happen when you are doing the same shops over and over again, and it's quite possible that either your accent or the way you shop might reveal you.

The thing is just by putting a programme in place, your employees' attitude becomes more focused and every single customer becomes as important as a mystery shopper, so they all get treated the same way.

The benefit is that when a mystery shopping programme is put in place in a positive way, everyone gets involved. Go back and read Why Mystery Shopping for more details on how you could set up your own programme, or if you want expert help, just get in touch with me as I've created a new service just for that Mystery Shopping DIY with me[17]

"Mystery Shop to celebrate success, Mystery Shop to identify your gaps, Mystery Shop to thrive in business" Claire Boscq-Scott

---

[17]https://busyqueenbee.com/services/mystery-shopping-diy-with-me

The light went off!

Gabrielle, my daughter, was six when I set up the business. She loved the idea of being a Mystery Shopper and she used to carry a little book and a pen when we were going shopping. She used to write the name of assistants in shops and what they did or said.

Once, we had a restaurant group who wanted to get their branches measure and was asked to bring my family with me. We arrived in the restaurant and as she loved being a little mystery shopper, I sent her to the toilets to check them out. She was gone a good 10 minutes and as I was about to come and see where she was, she re-appeared running back from the toilet and said: "Mum, mum, you won't believe what happened! I was on the toilet and the light went off, so I couldn't see anything. I was a bit scared and eventually managed to open the door and the light came back on".

You can imagine the situation: the toilet lights were activated by sensor. The door was tall enough to trigger it, but she wasn't. The lights went off until she managed to open the door again.

The point is what this group of restaurants did after this visit: they re-ajusted all of their toilets sensors so small people could also be picked up by the sensors. They also took it a step further, having had this feedback from a six year old girl. They revisited their 'young' customer experience, and suddenly increased their family's customs by 40%.

The benefit is Customer-centric businesses don't let their customers wander in search of information or help; instead, they provide customer experience excellence. They guide their customers through a carefully planned series of interactions called a customer journey.

A customer journey comprises experiences which are, in turn, made up of touch points — human, physical, sensory or communication, either in person or virtual — and which are influenced by factors like price, convenience and location. The implementation of the customer journey is dependent on your knowledge of exactly what your touch points are, and how well those touch points meet customer needs. You can/should do this on a smaller scale by focusing on a product line, division, or customer segment first, then move to another part of the business so you can build the full picture. Download a Retail Journey Canvas template, on the resources of the book webpage[18]

> The 'journey' is associated primarily with the physical interactions (behaviour) - contact strategy and reducing customer effort - whereas the 'experience' is the concept that deals primarily with how customers feel (emotion) with delighting customers' and creating distinct experiences.

---

[18]https://www.claireboscqscott.com/books/the-secret-diary-of-a-mystery-shopper/

Call centre

This was a mystery call I had to do - we have been working with this client for a long time now, and they had some new legislations that came in place and had trained their staff on the new requirements. This is was what the call would be measuring.

Overall, I had a very positive experience during the call with that company. After explaining my scenario, James, the adviser, asked what size package I intended to send and asked if it would be in a box. I said I was planning to send it in a suitcase and James later suggested that I should consider shrink wrapping the suitcase to avoid any labels coming off in the postage process.

Firstly, James explained the options of postal companies I could use, which they said would be suitable for items weighing up to the maximum of 30kg and no more than 1.5meters in length. He kindly informed me this would be suitable sizing for a suitcase and provided the postage cost for this service and that I couldn't send perfume or it may be confiscated. I then asked the speed of this delivery option and the adviser explained that, at present, they anticipate it taking 3-5 days, as there are currently delays and aren't able to guarantee next day delivery with this service. I then asked if there was a quicker option, to which James was able to explain the FedEx service. He continued with a very confident voice and informed me of the cost of this service, plus an additional courier fee. I asked about the speed difference and he initially said that it would be delivered as quickly as it can get there.

My only slight feedback would be that James did not provide me with a time frame to compare against the Parcel Force option, so I then questioned this and the adviser said they think it would take 1-2 days maximum. But he did provide information about taking the package and specifically asking for the other courier options. I felt very satisfied with the answers provided and the call was ended in a professional manner. Based on the service provided, I would have happily recommend the service to family and friends.

The point is being able to measure the legal aspect of the organisation is a part of the service deliver. If the employee gives the wrong information, the customer is going to find themselves in an annoying situation or could even be fined for something they thought they were doing right. It is key when you create a questionnaire that every aspect of your business is taken into consideration.

The benefit is on the phone, the product knowledge and the speed to deal with the customer is important. Most of all, the tone of the human voice changes when smiling. It is readily perceivable to the caller and it sets the tone for the rest of the call. It's been proven that a smile puts the caller at ease. Their mood then matches that of the person who answered the phone for the duration of the call. Being able to build rapport and increasing awareness for verbal communication when you don't see the person is a skill. You can teach your employees those skills, like mirroring the words used, the tone of voice and the speed of the conversation. These are all **NLP (Neuro Linguistic Programming) techniques**, which can be taught very easily to all your members of staff. You'll see an incredible difference in their communication skills, selling skills, complaint handling... Click here to see more details on NLP Training online course[19]

> "The quality of your communication shapes the quality of your life. Every cell in your being aligns with what you declare." — Niurka

---

[19]https://bqbcxinstitute.org/courses/become-a-certified-nlp-practitioner/

Video recording visit

With video recording visits, you have to know what you are doing. When shopping, you feel even more conscious of being under-cover with a hidden camera on your shirt, and even me - with years of experience with a camera - I am always a little more nervous. You have to get the right angle, you have to ensure your shirt doesn't move, and for us ladies, it's even harder to get the sirt to stay straight with our cleavage... you have to try not to move too fast or bend...

I was ready. I had set up my camera on my shirt and stopped a little earlier to check it had been turned on and it was working. I parked and came out of the car and re-adjusted myself before I walked toward the dealership.

As soon as I walked through the glass door, Bob, the Sales Executive, came out to attend to my custom. I know, car sales people have a reputation to be pushy and overselling. I have experienced this and just thinking about it makes me cringe. So Bob stood near me and started asking me lots of questions. The first question he asked me was, how did I want to feel when I imagine myself driving the car? Then, where was I going to drive the vehicle, and what were my favourite colours, and did I want manual or automatic, and have I driven one of those cars before, and did I like it? I wasn't put off by his questions and felt that he genuinely was trying to understand who I was, rather than trying to sell me anything he could get rid of!

He was very observant. When the topic came up, he already knew what type of car I was driving, as it was the only one parked in the customers' space and he had seen me driving in.

After qualifying my needs, Bob took me to a couple of cars which he thought would be suitable. From here, he was fully engaged. He was focused on my needs and explained everything. We discussed things like automatic parking, diesel or petrol, economic drive, air con, etc... I felt comfortable in his company and he knew what he talking about, but wasn't pushy or too selly...

I picked one of the cars as my preference and he then went into even more details about that particular option, as well as other specifications available in the same model. He said how much he liked that car, and how so many people go for the same option. He said it was a very trending and reliable car, easy to park, and low in maintenance and petrol too!

After telling me he could really see me in that car... He suggested a test drive which I declined for the moment. Finally he took me to David, his Business Manager, where we discussed parts exchange and various options of funding. We started with my preferred option, accounted for a particular deal (balloon) that guarantees a minimum value for the vehicle after full repayment. Upon which I would have 3 options. It also included a potential value for my present vehicle. On my way out David also mentioned an ongoing monthly payment for "Servicing".

Bob and David were most trustworthy. They both conveyed genuineness. I would have no reserves at all about doing business with them. For operational purposes, the only detail that did not go as perfect was the fact that the key to my car of choice could not be found, so I could not experience the car from the inside. I was kindly taken to the assistant's car instead for demonstration of features, and I even got a detailed email from the David, two hours after the visit.

The thing is the visit went very well and the footage was showed during their monthly meeting. Not only do the clients get a full report with their score but also they are able to use the film to review of all their sales team, and pin point what was very good and where it could have been improved. With the camera filming during the whole time, there is no complaint to be made from the employees' point of view. Of course, when the results are good, everyone is happy - when the results aren't great, the employees tent to be very defensive; it is the Fight or Flight response! They will argue that they didn't do this or that! With a camera, there are no arguments to be made, it's there in colour and live!

Please note that with the new data protection legislation, you must have it in your employees' contract that they might be filmed and that they agree to that. You also need to ensure that any other person on the film is being blurred to keep their identity anonymous... PLEASE CHECK with your local lesgislation when it comes to video-recording what you can and can't do, and make sure you are following legal advice as many countries do not permit it!

The benefit is right from the beginning, I felt the assistant was genuinely interested in me - in what I wanted and how I wanted to feel. This is such a key part of any sales experience. If you create a good rapport, if you are genuinely interested in your customers needs and you are able to **sell them the benefits** of your product first - in this instance, how you are going to feel driving that car - followed then by the features, then it's a winner. Download the exercise I created to do with your team which looks at Benefits V feature in the resources on the (book web-page)[https://www.claireboscqscott.com/books/the-secret-diary-of-a-mystery-shopper/]

Toilet check

This assignment was to measure the overall service of a restaurant. I checked the location and looked up what type of restaurant it was. It looked like an up-market trendy restaurant in a buzzing area of the city...

The day was set. The questionnaire to be followed was pretty straight forward, with sections on general approach, first impressions, order taken, friendliness and efficiency of the overall quality of the service, food rating, bill at the end - and of course, the toilets!

When a customer comes to your business for the first time, he takes a chance. He doesn't know if your products or services will be good. He hopes your service delivery will be pleasant, but he has no assurance that he will have a quality experience with your company.

Everybody knows how important first impressions are. It takes seven seconds for someone to make an opinion about you or your business, according to Shannon Kohn (2013); studies show that 55% of a person's opinion is driven by your physical appearance and first impressions: • 55% of people base their first impression on body anguage and personal appearance: the visual • 38% of people base their first impression on what you say: the vocal • 7% of people base their first impression on the words you use: the vocabulary

We arrived early, so there wasn't too many people in the restaurant. We were welcomed by Chantal. She smiled and asked if we had a reservation. I really needed to go to the toilet, so I told my partner to go and sit down first. The host took him to the table whilst I went to the toilet... I have a thing about the state of restaurants' toilets - my dad always said: 'your toilets will say a lot about the state of your kitchen!!'

When I walked in, the toilet smelt lovely - nice lighting, the chromes of the taps were shiny... But after that first good impression, I was surprised to turn my attention to an object left on the top of the sink just under the hand dryer... A recognisable shape. It was an adult toy. Ummmmm.... so much for making an unforgettable first impression!!

I had to go back to see Chantal and explained my discovery... as I couldn't say out loud what I found, I asked her to follow me to the toilet, so I could point out what needed to be removed. I am not sure which one of us was most embarrassed - her, or me... this must have made a great read too when I wrote up my report!!

The point is fast-paced work environments and complex tasks can often make it a challenge to pay close attention to the details of every element of your job performance. But overlooking details can sometimes be costly, detrimental to the quality of your work product, or in some cases, even dangerous or awkward! Developing your own Mystery Shopping programme will enable you to measure what is really important to you and your business. If you want to give it a go yourself, I have developed a new Mystery Shopping online training course[20] which takes you step by step so you can develop your own programme and roll it out yourself, without having the cost of using a professional company.

The benefit is for the true success of your ventures, **detailed oriented skills and caring for details are crucial.** An eye for precision and accuracy and a sense for diligence are qualities which are expected in order to deliver high quality service. Creating some standards, with specific checks and measurements, will help you find a consistency for all your members of staff - even those who clean the toilets.

---

[20]https://bqbcxinstitute.org/courses/mystery-shopping-online-training-course/

Customer experience is everyone's responsibility, not just a single department! Customer service must be an essential element of the culture of every company, and a good customer experience depends upon cross-departmental collaboration and accountability.

The Bad

What a difference a day makes ~ 24 little hours

I arrived at my hotel at 10.30am after leaving Kuwait on the 1am flight. The first thing I was faced with was trying to get my cases up the extremely narrow and steep stairs. Houses in Amsterdam are tall and narrow so culturally that is as it is, but nowhere on the website did it say not for people with disabilities or mobility problems. I have neither, but two heavy cases were enough of a difficulty. I should have realised something was not going to go well when Eva, the receptionist, argued that it does say no lift on website, well it didn't and I have since checked and it still doesn't.

Anyway, I sat and waited on the one and only small bench until some people checked out at 11am and a room was cleaned very quickly for me to check in. My experience of this "hotel" (even calling it a hotel is a misrepresentation) lasted exactly 3 hours. It ended with me being 'thrown out' for complaining that the electric sockets were hanging off the wall of my broom cupboard of a room, and the socket by the door sparked and crackled when you tried to charge anything e.g. phone or laptop.

My 'window' opened into the main body of the building with a lovely view of workmen's rubbish and silver foil clad pipes. No air just a skylight. I complained and was told if I didn't like it I could get out. The 'receptionist', shouted and screamed at me down the phone (I had to call on my mobile as there was no phone in the broom cupboard aka room) and then hung up on me when she had finished screaming, simply saying that I could just leave. I telephoned back from my mobile using what remaining battery I had as I couldn't charge anything, and Eva continued to scream at me and say that I had to pay for the one day I was there, which I refused so eventually she said that if I wanted a refund to come now. I went to the reception desk (which was in another building and down many stairs with my cases) and once there she continued to get very aggressive and kept screaming at me, at which stage I threatened to bring in the police to speak to her manager, but she claimed the manager wasn't there. I, eventually, got from her my 100% refund and struggled down the steep stairs with my cases once more, and as I was climbing slowly down the stairs she was behind me, at one point I thought that she would push me down the stairs, she was slight but much younger than me and screaming all the time. She pushed past me and walked out, leaving her reception desk and simply left the hotel. I was left shaking and crying on the street outside, a mixture of emotions fuelled by tiredness and anger. The owner of the cafe next door (a separate business) was the epitome of kindness. Not only did he welcome me in and gave me a coffee to calm me down but he went out of his way to find me another place to stay or I would have been on the streets as Amsterdam was completely fully booked on these dates because of it being a football weekend. Józefa Fawcett, International Trainer, Speaker & Coach[21]

The point is when something goes wrong what you will get is the customer will then go and tell all of their friends and family, post it on social media and within seconds thousands of people will be strongly warned NOT to book this hotel again! Now looking at the ratings on Trip Advisor, 6 said excellent while 91 said poor/terrible, this maybe an indication to the business owner that they have some big issues that need sorting out if they want to continue being open.

The benefit is having received that kind of feedback from a customer, it should trigger some action, assessing their standards, for quality of the service: the rudeness of that receptionist also surely needs to be addressed and some training on customer service

---

[21]http://jfistore.com

is essential. Also, a review of their safety within the bedroom facility was definitely necessary, as it is clear that a slight electric spark could one day cause a fire.

A solution to address this sort of situation is to put in place a process where you can **collect customer feedback**, it could be a manual little form that you leave in the room, or it could be an online form that you send after their stay. It is crucial to welcome feedback/ This is the only way you are going to learn and improve your services.

Assessing your customers and employees is now widely recognised as a vital input to any strategy for customer-focussed business performance improvement. Understanding customers' needs is the key to giving them an exceptional experience. If you are doing your own research on a limited budget, the best approach is to talk to existing customers and use simple surveys to gather information. Questionnaires are effective in getting feedback from existing customers. Respondents are usually happy to help as they can see a direct benefit. Remember to show you have acted on their feedback. More sophisticated methods, such as focus groups, are best left to the professionals (talk to me) or use research professionals who will provide an objective and balanced view; very often saving you time and money by getting it done professionally. Make sure you employ a company that is part of a professional body, such as MRS[22] or ESOMAR[23].

The key is to ask the right people the right questions and to make sure that you are asking enough people to get meaningful results. I know it seems obvious, but it isn't always the case. The world has changed. We know customers now have a voice; the voice of choice.

Your Most Unhappy Customers Are Your Greatest Source Of

---

[22]https://www.mrs.org.uk/
[23]http://www.esomar.org/

Learning" Bill Gates

Old ladies

I was doing some part time work at the time and one morning as I was getting ready, I noticed that I was very low on Foundation cream. At the time, I was using a very known brand so during my lunch hour I rushed to a department store to stock up.

The shop was buzzing, music was playing, and I loved the smell as I walked through the beauty department. I went towards the counter as I had purchased products from this brand several times before. I started looking around the dipslays.

I had been there for a few minutes browsing and couldn't find what I wanted, no one approached me to ask if they could help, so as I looked around for someone. I noticed the assistant I usually went to was not on duty. After browsing for another few minutes but not finding the product, I approached a young lady for assistance. Jennie was pleasant, she smiled and acknowledged me, she had a lovely foreign accent, was very well dressed and turned to help me straight away. I explained that I wanted another bottle of my favourite foundation but could not find it.

Jennie said if I took a seat, she would test all the ranges on me. I responded that unfortunately, I did not have time but I had noticed a range that seemed to offer good coverage so picked the tester up and asked if I could try it.

Within seconds, Jennie turned round to me, looked at the bottle I had picked up and took it off from my hands and said: "No, that range is not for old ladies"!

To say, I was mortified, would be an understatement. I made my excuses and left. Ummmm….

The thing is I understand that Jennie was not English native and therefore may not realise that what she said was offensive, but it was also the way she said it and how she reacted which shocked me and made me feel the rush to run out of the place for being told I was old and embarrassed that other people would have heard too!

The benefit is employees working for you could come from any part of the world, any ethnic, any social economic background, and it brings colours and diversity. However, it is really key for a **etiquette training** to be done before the staff are left on their own on the shop floor. What exactly do you want them to do? How do you require them to behave? Show them your expectations so they can meet your standards. A training strategy to run for the whole year will empower your staff, not just on hard skills but on essential skills (I hate the word soft skills). Train them on the core principles of being a caring person, give them the confidence in selling, building rapport and knowing what to say and what not to say! More details on our CX online training programmes[24]

> "'Train people well enough so they can leave, treat them well enough so they don't want to." Richard Branson.

---

[24]https://bqbcxinstitute.org/cx-programmes/

Receiving a Mystery Shop report

The assignment was to measure the service in a deli shop for one of the grocery stores in my area.

The standard requirements of this shop was to check the customer service at the deli counter in that grocery store. As I approached the counter, you could hear Jamie speaking to another co-worker about how unfair his evaluation had been the previous month from a secret shopper. He was going on and on and on about how this was unfair, though he did not say what they 'accused' him of!

Remember, I am standing right there in line waiting to be served. So who do I get to wait on me, but Jamie...

I was tempted to instruct him on the proper way to not get a bad evalution but decided against it, this wasn't my place, a Mystery Shopper must report objectively without being judgmental, unless your personal opinion is particularly asked - so that's what I had to do.

I followed my guidelines and placed my order. Unfortunately, Jamie continued his rant with the other associate whilst serving me then handed me the order without even looking at me, acknowledging me, or asking if there would be anything else he could get me.

I think you know how this report went as for customer service. I tried to keep it neutral as best I could but his attitude gave him yet another bad evaluation!

The point is it is really important to be very open and transparent when starting a Mystery Shopping programme. This assistant had obviously not been given feedback in a constructive way in which he could actually benefit from the feedback; but he didn't see that. Instead, he saw it as a reprimand rather than a benefit.

The benefit is Mystery Shopping is, of course, used to celebrate success and identify gaps. Actively **promote the Mystery shopping programme with your employees** by:

• Being very clear that the purpose of the mystery shopping programme is NOT to criticise, assign blame, or publicly embarrass anyone, and the results of the mystery shops will be used for improvement purposes and not to bash anyone over the head!
• Aligning company-wide focus on improving the customers' experiences
• Sharing exactly what types of questions will be on the mystery shop. You are only giving them what you are expecting of them so give them the tools to do a great job
• Sharing the results of each visit with the whole team. Discuss, analyse and empower your team to act differently
• Encouraging positive buy-in from customer-facing associates by offering some kind of reward to those who get exceptionally high scores on their shops. It could be a monetary reward or just a picture on the wall for being employee of the month.

If the benefits of a mystery shopping programme are communicated effectively, all employees should embrace mystery shops as an irreplaceable way to help them succeed by truly understanding what their customers experience. Every shop should be seen as an opportunity to more deeply understand exactly what customer delight-driving behaviours look and sound like, and every shop should be used for recognition and/or for positive, constructive coaching.

"Teach your employees the core principles for being a caring employee so that they can thrive in your business and in their life; C.A.R.E, be congruent, be accountable, be resilient and emotionally intelligent..." Claire Boscq-Scott

United breaks more than just guitars

OK, this is another true story and most of you would have heard about it! I have to say United Airlines is the airline who keeps on giving by dragging their customers out of the plane... **"We don't beat our competitors, but we do beat our customers"**

When I started developing my training sessions, "United Breaks Guitars"[25] was one of my favorite 'bad' services story. Here is a protest song by Canadian musician Dave Carroll and his band, Sons of Maxwell. It chronicles a real-life experience of how his guitar was broken during a trip on United Airlines in 2008, and the subsequent reaction from the airline. The song became an immediate YouTube and iTunes hit upon its release in July 2009 and a public relations embarrassment for the airline. Within 4 days of the video being posted online, United Airlines' stock price fell 10%, costing stockholders about $180 million in value. To date millions of people viewed his video, listened to his song over and over again. Since the incident, Carroll has been in great demand as a speaker on customer service. On one of his trips as a speaker, United Airlines lost his luggage... oh dear!

However, it was bad enough to have broken the guitar of this singer, but United Airline went a step further in the bad service stories when the video footage of the incident which occurred at Chicago's O'Hare International airport in 2017 of a passenger being dragged out of the plane was shared on social media and went viral in an astonishing amount of time. This prompted outrage globally, resulting in a loss of $1 billion in company total market value, just

---

[25]https://www.youtube.com/watch?v=5YGc4zOqozo

because this doctor wanted to go home to treat some patient and didn't want to leave his seat!

Shares in United Continental Holdings fell on Tuesday as the Company continued to draw fierce criticism for violently removing a passenger from an overbooked United Airlines flight so staff could take his seat. Shares recovered somewhat towards the end of the day to close the session 1.15 per cent lower. United Continental Holdings was also the second biggest faller on the S&P 500 index. The world went crazy about United Airlines throwing this passenger off the plane.

This thing is... I am really struggling to find any positiveness to that Company. It's unacceptable to be unempathetic to customers and not trying to help even though it's the Companies' fault. The customer assistant maybe was having a bad day and decided not to help Dave with his guitar. But it's a worse story when you are removing a man with blood flowing down his chin, from your plane. I don't know about you, but I will think twice before booking with United Airline and if I had to, I would always have this thought in the back of my mind, what if they are going to drag me out today!

The benefit is well, I guess, there is always a lesson to learn from any story and the moral of that one is, never, ever, ever drag your customers out of your business! **"Treat others how you want to be treated."** this saying goes far beyond simply being kind to people, or going out of your way to be available or helpful to those in need. The individual nature of disrespect makes it particularly challenging to preempt— you never really know what someone will take as disrespectful, so the easiest way to prevent the disrespect trigger from being pulled is to think in this way. Do the things that are likely to make most people feel respected. Being polite is the first and easiest way to treat your customers with respect, because customer service is just as simple as basic politeness. Say, 'Please,' say 'thank you', smile and ensure you make eye contact. There is nothing difficult there, it is just basic simple courtesy.

I would have hoped that United Airlines would have taken this incident very seriously and repair the damage done by their actions and was able to assess the situation and develop new procedures. For example, when their planes are full, if it was a case of urgency, they might look for someone in the plane who would be happy to travel on a later flight and be compensated for it, giving extra care at the airport which may keep their customers happy and cause them to continue flying with them.

> "Show respect to people who don't even deserve it; not as a reflection of their character, but as a reflection of yours." Dave Willis

Nail & fish nightmare

I arrived in the morning of the visit to get my nails and fish spa done. As I walked into the shop there was a lady being looked after and it took a few seconds for another assistant to come from the kitchen and approach me.

The assistant asked what I had booked and if I had had a fish spa treatment before. I explained it was the Valentines Day offer and said yes, but it was my first time here at this particular salon. She suggested I sat down by the reception and I should take my shoes off. She then went off towards the kitchen and asked if I wanted a drink. She went to put a bucket of hot water on top of a little step and she pointed it out to me and said I should put my feet in the water first before I put them in the fish tank. I walked bare foot across the shop and tried to get from the bucket to sit down and move my feet in the tank, this really isn't a practical way to do it. No-one came to ask me if I needed anything once during the whole time. I had to shout out for someone to come and get the tea bag out of my cup, because there was nowhere else to put it.

The treatment was advertised as 15 minutes, but after just 10 minutes the assistant came and asked me to remove my feet so she could dry them and I could put my shoes back on. But my feet were still wet, there was no towel on the floor so the floor was wet and I had to ask for another towel, to which she curtly replied, "pick one up from above your head". I was given the nail varnish colours but there wasn't any dark browns or dark reds, I asked if they had any others and was told no. I then said could I have a French Manicure, to which she said yes, but it will be another £5.00. Once I finished putting my shoes on, I went towards the manicure table. I suggested I could pay now before the manicure and she went toward the reception desk and asked me for £25.00. I then thought oh, she isn't charging me for the additional fee, that's a nice touch.

The assistant started to remove my nail varnish at 11.46am. Admittedly I did have 2 different colour nail varnishes on top of each other, however after 40 minutes trying to remove the varnish I asked if I could help her to remove bits behind the nail. She gave me the cotton wool and stood up to go into the kitchen with the other assistant.

They both started talking, then it went quiet, then they started laughing out loud. I couldn't help but keep thinking they were talking about me. By then, I felt very embarrassed by the situation. She returned to ask which colour I wanted, I said French Manicure, she said my nails were discoloured and I would be better going for a colour. As mentioned, there was no dark colours and I wanted French and she then said I had to pay the £5 extra.

By now, I just wanted to leave the shop, I picked up any colour and I allowed her to start on the varnishing. It was then 12.30pm and I was due to meet with a friend at that time, who came in and waited whilst the assistant finished putting the varnish on. She had to put 3 layers on as the varnish seemed very fluid to me, but the assistant said all of these varnish colours were like this. When finished she just got up and walked to the kitchen, she came back to say goodbye as we were almost outside the door. I was in the shop for 1 hour and 15 minutes. I was in the fish tank for 10 minutes when I was expecting 15, the nail polish was acceptable however the assistant wasn't engaging at all. She made me feel very awkward. The overall experience wasn't one I would like to experience again. I felt left to my own devices then embarrassed in thinking the assistants were talking about me in the kitchen. The shop was so cold I was shivering. Following this visit I won't be returning to that Spa.

The thing is Service is intangible - customers' recollection of the transaction is their reality, their attitudes & feelings, their physiological state. It will help them to decide if they want to do business with you again. We seek pleasure & avoid pain, so we tend to return to companies that meet or exceed our requirements & avoid the ones that cause pain.

The benefit is Customers will have their own **expectations** of what they expect you to do. Their expectations are rarely passed on to you. However, if you don't meet them, the customer may conclude that you have failed. Once you have identified those expectations they can be carefully handled, changed or adjusted. This assistant made no effort to try to meet my expectations, never mind exceed them, I may be wrong, but I am sure that if any other customer had been given that kind of service and attitude, this may be the reason why this shop has closed down now! **To create a delightful emotional experience you need to fulfill the basic customer expectations, meet the obvious customer expectations and strive to exceed customer expectations.**

'The key is to set realistic customer expectations, and then not to just meet them, but to exceed them...' - Richard Branson

The Exceptional

Can you steal Jewellery?

Ok, so that was a first, I just received an email from my clients, a large Jewellers, who had just finished a big safety and theft training with their staff and wanted us to go and try to steal something from one of their shops.

Wow, ok, this was taking Mystery Shopping into a whole new dimension as this could have secondary implications we had to think about before the visit.

What happens if I get caught?
What happens if the alarm is raised and the employee calls the police?
What happens if I get filmed on CCTV?

Ok, you see where I am coming from, but after a good conversation with the client and arranging all the possibilities, I agreed to perform the visit.

We had been running this programme for several months, so the questionnaire for the client hadn't changed; it was the briefing which was making the whole visit much more interesting.

The day arrived and I walked into the shop. There was only one couple discussing with the assistant a pair of earrings, so I went and had a little browse. When Shirley, the assistant, finished with the couple, she approached me in a very friendly manner. She was wearing a branded uniform with her name badge and a particularly nice necklace and she asked if I needed any help.

I had noticed the cabinet at the back of the shop. This would be the easiest for me to try to get my hands on one of the items. Anything would have done... so I asked Shirley if I could see a necklace on the second shelf. As I said, I really loved her necklace and she was happy to say it was one of the perks of the job as she was getting a very good discount.

As she opened the cabinet, the phone rang, and I thought wow, this is my chance. She had walked away from the cabinet without closing it and I thought I would have only seconds to get it, my heart was beating very fast and I felt as if everyone was staring at me; my hands were shaking... I quickly went towards the door to open it, when I felt her body moving me to the side as she raced to close the cabinet. My face was so red from embarrasement. I said I was just going to take a look at the necklace and she said she was sorry she was going to take the call and then come back to me so I could try it with her.

OK, at that point, I was a little annoyed that she decided to take the call before serving me, but I knew that she had done a very god job in securing the cabinet before doing something else. A few seconds later, Shirley came back and apologised for the wait and said she had been expecting that call all morning; it was personal but really important and she seemed genuinely sorry. She went back to the cabinet, got the necklace out, closed the cabinet behind her and there was no chance for me whatsoever to steal anything with this assistant on duty. She was very thorough; never left me after that incident and I ended up buying it so I could actually finish the visit.

The client was very pleased with the results and we performed several similar visits in other branches to check the consistency of the security and they all went very well indeed.

The point is this was a bold visit and it could have ended up in a more awkward way, but the assistant obviously had listened carefully to the training and recognised her responsibility within the organisation.

The benefit is mystery shopping is measuring the service delivery, however to gain the most information from the results use briefings/scenarios to **align with your training strategy**.

When I worked at Disney World, we were not actually allowed to get into the parks without having done our full week at Mickey Mouse University! Why would you send your employees on the shop floor or answering phone calls without training them! This just baffles me when I see those poor employees who have been in the organisation for days and feel completely like a fish out of water! Training your employees isn't just a need, it is simply a necessity.

The importance of training your employees - both new and experienced - cannot be over-emphasised. Effective training of employees results in employees who:

- Know what they're doing
- Save time
- Have a good feeling about the company; it shows that they care
- Get off to a good start
- Reduce employee turnaround
- Boost confidence
- Increase performance
- Creates Sales growth (of course)

Training simply refers to the process of acquiring the essential skills required for a certain job. It targets specific goals, for instance understanding a process and operating a certain machine or system. Those are hard skills and are related to specific technical knowledge.

Whereas 'soft skills' are the traits that make you a good employee, such as etiquette, communication and listening and getting along with other people. Those are Essential Skills, not soft! Employees need to master those skills when they are facing their customers, regardless of the type of contact that you have with customers, whether it is over the phone, face-to-face, in a restaurant or shop, in an office or financial institution, or in the entertainment or tourist industries. Good customer service skills helps everybody.

> "Stop spending money on marketing and advertising if you don't spend money on training" Claire Boscq-Scott

Thank you card!

This was a visit we asked a Mystery Shopper to perform, let's call her Jean, The visit was to a retailer and she had to purchase a pair of jeans.

When Jean walked in, the store was very attractive, music was playing, there was good lighting and everything looked in order. There was two members of staff who were dealing with stock and one at the counter. Jean had a little walk around and as soon as she returned a second time near the jeans, Harriet, the assistant, approached and asked if she needed help. The shopper said that she would like to buy some jeans, and Harriet pointed to the area where all the skinny jeans were and asked if she had any particular style in mind. As soon as Harriet realised Jean did not like skinny jeans, she totally left those aside and concentrated on the flared ones.

Harriet asked if she wanted something for summer or was she looking for winter? She also said that she might need high heeled shoes and offered to find her some if she wished to try and see how they would look like on.

Harriet had a naturally kind nature that made my shopper feel appreciated and looked after. With the pair of jeans Jean tried on she went to Harriet to show her and ask how they fitted. Jean asked for the size above just to check the fit, Harriet immediately brought them and when our shopper tried those on and she asked Harriet's honest opinion. Harriet was kind enough to leave it up to me to decide but she indicated that the size 10 looked better. When my shopper mentioned about having to lose some weight Harriet very kindly and genuinely said that she was perfect and not to think differently!

Harriet was a natural with her customer service skills and Jean was so satisfied with the service, with her confidence and knowledge, she said she had an eye for clothing. Harriet explained how the jeans would fit and length of them as my shopper said to her she was not very tall like her and asked what she could wear them with.

Anyway, the visit finished, Jean did buy the pair of jeans and kept them and entered the visit in the system and sent us a little note to say how fantastic the assistant had been. In fact she was so impressed with her that she returned the next day and gave her a little thank you card!!!!...

The point is As you can imagine we were quite taken aback that Jean returned to the store with a 'Thank you card' for the assistant! We had to remind her that being a Mystery shopper, you need to blend in as 'normal customers' and she would have been noticed with her act of kindness. Once the assistant is shown the report she will remember her. A shopper can say in the review how helpful the assistant was and believe me she will be recognised by her manager, but not return and give her a card! We had to inform the client that this took place and of course we couldn't use this shopper for any further visits to this client in the future, but the good intention was there.

The benefit is Ok, so my shopper got a bit carried away, but imagine how the assistant would have felt receiving a thank you card from one of her clients. Being grateful to our employees goes a long way to make employees feel valued. When you fight for your team, your team will fight for you. Celebrating success doesn't mean that you have to give them more financially. When developing your Employee Experience, an **Employee Reward & Recognition programme** is amazing to increase employee loyalty. There are many non-financial rewards you can give that will help, such as giving respect and praise, having an employee of the month, being flexible when they need time off, listening to their suggestions and feedback or just a simple thank you will go a long way to make your employees feel valued. Why not make this recognistion even more public and enter into Industry awards? Check out The Wow Awards[26] and mention my name!!

> "We measure success by the way we touch the lives of people."
> Bob Chapman, CEO of Barry-Wehmiller

---

[26]https://www.thewowawards.co.uk/

How much did I spend??

With new clients, I would most of the time perform the first visit. I want to check the environment myself; I want to check that there isn't anything we should be aware of in advance and also it's a great way for me to familiarise myself close up and personal with the company to understand where they are.

This was a new client, we were excited to be working with them as a new Spa Salon. After we developed the programme with the client, I assigned myself the first visit. Well, with a free two-hours' treatement, with massage, facial, and finished with an indian head massage, I just had to do it of course!!

There were a lot of criterias to remember, the client was very specific with the journey, such as how did I feel before, during and after the treatment?

As I walked in, I was welcomed by a beautiful aroma straight away. The reception area looked very attractive, there were some nice display cabinets and warm purple colours with gold paintings on the wall and a crystal chandelier. It looked luxurious and I felt as if I was in heaven. The receptionist took a few details from me and shown me around the Spa. She explained the facilities and we went to the changing room where she gave me a robe and slippers and gave me a key for my locker. She asked me to get changed and go and relax in the relaxation room until I got called.

Everything was sparkling, I had a good look in the showers and the toilets, the changing room was tidy, hair dryer, perfume, hair mousse and perfume were on display for customers to use; it really felt luxurious.

I walked to the relaxation room where I was welcomed by Ellie, who took me to a bed. She brought me some 'cucumber water' and asked if I wanted some natural tea. I said yes, of course, as I sat there, I looked around and an atmospere of peace and tranquility was all around, the colours choosen were perfect, incense was burning, a calm piano music was playing in the background and when Ellie gave me the tea, my five senses got all connected at once and I felt so good and so relaxed; 'I must be on another planet, I thought'. Hang on there, get back on this planet you have some work to do girl!!

After another five minutes of relaxation a lady called Bella came to get me. Again, very friendly, well presented in a simple brown tunic, we walked towards the treatment room. She introduced herself and explained what was going to happen, how it was going to happen and she asked if I had any injuries, and if I wanted something specific looked at. Really it was unbelievable how thorough she was. Bella started the treatment, and as she was going along she was telling me what she was using and what were the benefits. It was so amazing I didn't want that treatment to finish. But it did, and then Bella showed me all the products she used, and how this is good for this and that.

I loved everything and bought over £200 worth of products, WHAT?? how did that happen? I know the selling techniques, I should have not bought all those products but I did, because Bella was so good with everything, so knowledgeable, so genuinely kind in showing me what was best for me. I was under her spell and bought everything she suggested!

The thing is this visit for me was exceptional from every point. One big thing you hear me talk a lot about is the **environment and how it affects its employees and its customers**; Your environment has a lot to do with how you feel, and how you feel has a lot to do with how productive you are. Neuroscientists across the globe have studied images of the brain in action and placed emotion in the driver's seat, asserting that thinking is emotion-based, and while emotions form the basis of thoughts, the five senses – sight, sound, smell, taste and touch – fuel those emotions, wielding the power to persuade, relax and heal.

"Emotions affect awareness, consideration, persuasion, recall and loyalty in the marketplace," says Dan Hill, author of Emotionomics: Winning Hearts and Minds (Adams Business & Professional, 2007).

Sensory design has earned its place in high-end spas and resorts; but today, hospitals, airports, retail environments and corporate offices alike embrace the senses to forge brand identity while creating inviting environments.

One of the most powerful senses, smell, can trigger associations and draw upon fond memories of other smells. Customers' olfactory sense augment the Customer Experience. This is all part of the subconscious Experience. According to Rachel Herz, professor of psychiatry and human behaviour and author of the book "The Scent of Desire", a smell is just a scent until a person associates it with a specific experience. After the association, the smell becomes a representation of that experience in the mind of the person.

Businesses should consider the power of this link and choose a smell that associates their Experience with your brand. Consider how you can use smells to transport, transcend, and tweak your Customers' Experience. I know the sense of smell is so powerful, I even created my own perfume called Eau d'abeille[27] to enhance the business environment, and I am not the only one. I remember at Disney World, we use to add French bread essence to the air conditioning system to attract customers and the queues were never ending at the bakery... Check out Hilton Hotels, McDonald, Rolls Royce and many others, even better why not creating your own Signature Fragrance!

From the moment I walked into the Spa, I felt at home, I didn't want to leave. How it smelt, how it felt, what I could see, touch, hear was all connecting to my five senses and making me feel good.

---

[27] https://www.claireboscqscott.com/eau-dabeille-perfume/

Look at ways you can achieve this high level of connection through the environment, by using the five senses and using old chinese techniques such as **Feng Shui**, the Chinese Art of placement. If you need some help with that, let me know, as I am a practitioner in this pseudoscientific traditional practice and I would love to come and do a discovery audit in your organisation!

The client was very happy with the report. They also had a smile on their face when I told them that I managed to spend more on their products than what they were paying me for the visit. We were able to continue the programme and we also used this assistant to train the others who had not received such excellent feedback

The benefit is employee selection and recruiting the right people for the right job is important so make sure you employ 'Radiators' not 'Drains'. This must be top of your priority list of your employees' experience. It is not always easy for some HR managers as they would say, but in the long term, surely it makes more sense to have no-one in a position who is the wrong employee. It will save you a lot of time and money for sure. **Hire for attitude and train for skill** employ people who are enthusiastic, who are aligned with your company's values, who will in the long term be engaged, and will work together to achieve the higher mission of the company. You can train everything else. An exercise that I love doing when I am training is the Personal Behaviour exercise, download the exercise in the resources on the book webpage[28] this exercise is very powerful to understand your employee behviours' style and how they will all work together as a team in a more harmonious way, as they understand each other and can communicate with each other better.

> "You don't hire for skills, you hire for attitude. You can always teach skills." - Simon Sinek

When the CEO behaves badly!

Have you heard of the 'Ratner affect' or 'Doing a Ratner'? Gerald Ratner inherited his father's business in 1984 and in 6 years transformed it from a small jewellers into a multimillion dollar empire.

He made it so successful that it seemed every British high street had a Ratner's store or one of the associated companies he had bought up.

People loved his store because it offered affordable products to the working class. In fact it was generally known as the place where working-class boys bought rings for working-class girls.

Life was going well for Ratner, who had expensive cars, houses, boats, women - and he frequented many high society events and was rubbing shoulders with the Prime Minister, Margaret Thatcher, at Number 10.

Yes life was good until the fateful day when he was guest speaker at the Institute of Directors on April 23, 1991, attended by over 6000 business people and journalists.

For reasons only known to himself Ratner decided to undo not only his entire life but his empire in less than 10 seconds. When asked how was it possible for his Company to be selling a sherry decanter for the extraordinary price of £4.95 he answered, to the amazement of his audience and his shareholders, with the following explanation: **"Because it's total crap."**

To make sure that he really made a good job of it he also stated this about his Company: 'We sold a pair of earrings for under a pound, which is cheaper than a shrimp sandwich from Marks and Spencer, but propbably wouldn't last as long.'

The point is Gerald lost his playboy lifestyle as well as his job. But this was a harsh lesson learnt, that no matter who you are, where you are, you are representing your company. Some people say that any press is good press but on this occasion negative press was certainly not good for anyone so why did he do it? I doubt he intended to do it; 5 words which changed his life for ever: goodbye job, sports car, luxury lifestyle, etc. He lost everything. As you can guess the media had a field day with this and ran the story so many times that any working-class boy buying his working-class girlfriend 'crap' from Ratners would not be "getting lucky tonight'. Additionally the Company's shares dropped £500 million in a matter of days.

The benefit is Every word yourself or your employees use can have a huge impact on the business. Now the Company had to do a Phoenix and rename themselves 'Signet Group' in 1993. The Company has made quite a turnaround in financial performance and attitude since the early 1990s.

Terry Burman, CEO since March 2000, speaks of product quality only in the most positive terms, and he has made "continuous improvement": a mantra among his managers and salespeople. Signet boosted profits up 27 percent (at constant exchange rates), to £53.9 million ($97 million).

Terry Burman says: Our recent results are very gratifying, but we pride ourselves on taking a long-term view. Over five years compound annual growth in earnings per share is 15 percent, and comparable-store sales are up 5.8 percent. That's what we're most proud of, because we are passionate about making continuous improvements in the business. We are constantly testing new ideas, rolling out those that test successfully and continuously revisiting all the key disciplines: display, merchandise, advertising, operations etc to sustain that performance.

What an amazing story how a probably very unintentional comment destroyed a brand in seconds and after sheer perseverence, dedication and refocus on their story, they managed to become the world's largest jewellery retailer by sales: No. 1 in the U.K., where it operates 600 stores under the Ernest Jones, H. Samuel and Leslie Davis names, and No. 2 behind Zale Corp. in the U.S., where it runs 1,126 stores, including Jared, J.B. Robinson and Kay Jewellers.

> "The tongue is a small thing, but what enormous damage it can do." James 3:5

A new hairdo

So, here we are and just this morning I was talking to a friend of mine, Jessica, and she was telling me about her experience... she fancied a new hairdo and as we know, ladies, letting someone new cut your hair is a BIG deal, so she booked somewhere which had been recommended to her and had her appointment at 10am. Jessica got there a little early, as you do, just to be sure to be on time. She was welcomed by a young girl, who wasn't wearing a name badge, and who asked her to sit down and wait.

10.10am nothing, 10.15am nothing, 10.20am still no-one has approached her, so Jessica gets up and goes to the reception desk and asked when will she be looked after? The young girl at the desk says, "Well I'm not too sure, as he hasn't arrived yet, I will try to ring him!" What?? #doesanyonecare

My friend was quite shocked that no-one had tried to call him earlier since he was due to start at 10am and it took her intervention for someone to do something. Jessica stayed at the desk whilst the young girl tried to ring. Home number no answer; mobile no answer. The young girl says, "I will try the boyfriend". At last someone answers and says, "he isn't feeling well and is not coming to work today"! What? #howrude

The young girl just didn't know where to put herself. By now my friend was quite irritated and was about to leave the salon when the Manageress, Emma came to reception and questioned what was happening. She said, "What? What do you mean he isn't coming in, why hasn't anyone told me about this?" #awkward

Emma couldn't apologise enough and was obviously really embarrassed about the whole situation. She took my friend to oneside and said to her she would take care of her herself. She sat her down, got her a coffee, chatted about her hair and what she wanted to do. She washed her hair herself and even gave her a head massage. When she finished with the whole hairdo Emma gave Jessica a discounted price and couldn't have done anything more to please her.

The point is Emma turned a poor situation, which could have cost her reputation into a great experience. Yes, things happen,yes, staff don't turn up, yes, your dog may have died today and all of those personal situations shouldn't have any impact on your customers. When Emma said if you want to come back to the stylist you booked in the first place, you will get a discount, Jessica said, "NO-WAY, I will come back to him, if he can't be trusted to ring you to come to work how can I trust him with my hair, but I would definitely come back to you".

The benefit is Wow, my friend was impressed, turning an unhappy customer into a happy one, who will go and tell all of their friends and family which is **how to create raving fans**. Prioritise creating raving fans to transform your business. Really get to know your customers. Give advice rather than information. Deliver more than you promise to create raving fans. Move your customers to a better place. Reward your best customers to turn them into raving fans. Raving fans are free marketers: they are your advocate, they will come back to you, recommend you, never leave you and of course they will increase your profitability. It is as simple as that!

> "The worst thing you can do is meet expectations one time, fall short another, and exceed every now and then. I guarantee you'll drive your customers nuts and into the hands of the competition the first chance they get." Ken Blanchard.

The End

The BIG vision

So, yes I love being a Mystery Shopper because it is incredible to be able to help businesses improve their service delivery in a very effective way. I also loved Mystery shopping because I was getting paid to get massages, nails done, eat in restaurants and sleep in fabulous hotels, who wouldn't want that??

Okay, okay, it's not as easy as I make it sound, there is a lot of work before, during and after to ensure that we are giving clients the best results. Results can make a difference to their business, to their employees and of course their customers. And this is my mission, I live to inspire global businesses to thrive by delivering exceptional customer experiences in measuring and improving employees' performances, and bringing more care into what they do, alluring senses to connect with employees and customers on an emotional level.

I love bringing a more holistic approach to Employee and Customer eXperience, empowering leaders to bring more care into what they do, creating sensorial experiences, enhancing their environments, increasing their employees' engagement and loyal customers.

However, my much bigger vision is just like the bees who dedicate every second of their 150 days' life to collecting pollen for the greater good of the hive but moreso for the greater good of our ecosystem, that makes all life on the planet possible, if I can inspire businesses to deliver exceptional customer experiences, the businesses will thrive, the local economy will thrive too, prospering with happy employees, happy customers and a happy community.

We need to change the way we do business. We are entering

into a new Era. It is time to evolve into the next phase of higher consciousness whereby businesses become accountable for their environment, their employees and their customers.

There is a real shift in culture that needs to happen. We need to ensure that every step we take, every move we make, is focussed on the customer. Not just your external customers either, those who come through the front doors, it is crucial to look after your internal customers too, those who walk through your back doors, as they are the ones who are going to look after the customers who walk through the front door -if you see what I mean!

Be a change Leader, to grow and change some of your old habits, to become the 'New Era leaders' in the 21st Century:

- by nurturing a 'Caring Service Culture'
- by creating a better environment for your employees to feel happy to come to work everyday
- by developing unforgettable customer experiences every time they walk through your doors
- by genuinely 'caring' for the customers and the employees to become central to all processes

So together you can deliver consistently exceptional customer experiences, resulting in exponential growth and thriving businesses through a Caring Service Culture.

> "Your employees are your white cells and your customers are your red cells, they make the blood stream of your business; if you have no customers, you have no business." Claire Boscq-Scott

The End

There is a French proverb who says, "Jamais deux sans trois" ('never two without three)... when I wrote my first book Thrive with the Hive[29] I said, I will never do that again... and so two years later, I did and wrote Thriving by Caring[30]. After that, I have had this Secret Diary book in the back of my mind for quite a while, but never done anything with it. I even started writing a series of blogs and when I announced it to my clients, several felt they might be too many conflicts and I didn't want to upset anyone, so I stopped.

But this book isn't about naming and shaming, this book is here to help.

Customer Experience is simple when you do it consistently well, the only way to do that is to assess, develop, implement/train and measure regularly. It is a virtual cycle just like the bees doing their Waggle Dance...

If like the bees, I keep communicating ideas, tips, inspirations, ways to buzz in your business to deliver better customer service, to build better relationships with your internal and external customers and ultimately to grow your profitability, I will have done my job!

---

[29]https://www.claireboscqscott.com/books/thrive-with-the-hive/
[30]https://www.claireboscqscott.com/books/thriving-by-caring/

Thank you

The last few months have certainly challenged me, my 'raison de vivre', my whys, my mission and purpose in life, but somehow despite everything that is happening in the world, I know deep down within me that I am on the right path and this is what I am meant to be doing.

I would not have been able to go through this period without my two amazing children, Luc and Gabrielle and their support, their kindness, their love and so much positive energy. Even if I live far away from my family, their moral support has been invaluable and I feel very lucky to be surrounded by people here on this little island in the middle of the Channel, who are here through the good times and the bad times, who believe in me - and I am very grateful to you all, you know who you are!!

A BIG thank you to my talented niece, who is based in Canada, and has got, like her great grandfather, a gift. The gift of drawing, so when I started writing the book and I was telling her my little idea, she came up straightaway with the 'little me' illustration you have seen throughout the book. She is so very clever, so if anyone wants to get in touch with her, here are her details:

Agathe Illustration[31]
Facebook: @agatheillustration[32]
Instagram: @agathe.b_illustration[33]

---

[31]https://agatheboscq1.wixsite.com/agathebillustration
[32]https://www.facebook.com/agathebillustration/
[33]https://www.instagram.com/agathe.b_illustration/

Customer service is so simple: with a positive, pro-active, engaging approach, when you give your internal customers the right tools, there is no reason why they wouldn't deliver exceptional customer service before, during and after to your external customers, so in return they will buy from you, they will return to you and recommend you.

www.ingramcontent.com/pod-product-compliance
Lightning Source LLC
Chambersburg PA
CBHW070503220526
45467CB00002B/541